AF334496

THE WOOLLY MAMMOTH & THE ASIAN ELEPHANT

by Jason M. Burns

Full Tilt Press
42964 Osgood Road
Fremont, CA 94539
readfulltilt.com
Full Tilt Press publications may be purchased for educational, business, or sales promotional use.

All internet sites appearing in back matter were available and accurate when this book was sent to press.

ISBN: 978-1-62920-764-3 (hardcover)

ISBN: 978-1-62920-791-9 (ePUB eBook)

ISBN: 978-1-62920-797-1 (PDF eBook)

Editorial Credits

Editor: Mari Bolte, Meghan Gottschall, and Michelle Parkin

Copyeditor: Kelley Barth

Designer: Sara Radka

Image Credits
page 3: ©Orla / Getty Images; page 3: ©gnomeandi / Getty Images; page 3: ©Bruce Levick / Getty Images; page 3: ©LEONELLO CALVETTI / Getty Images; page 4: ©Nerthuz / Getty Images; page 5: ©VICTOR HABBICK VISIONS/SCIENCE PHOTO LIBRARY / Getty Images; page 7: ©Nick Everett / Getty Images; page 9: ©Morphart Creation / Shutterstock; page 10: ©msan10 / Getty Images; page 10: ©bortonia / Getty Images; page 11: ©clipartdotcom / Getty Images; page 12: ©Aunt_Spray / Getty Images; page 13: ©Yuri_Arcurs / Getty Images; page 14: ©Daniel Eskridge / Getty Images; page 15: ©Deanna DeShea / 500px / Getty Images; page 17: ©John Harper / Getty Images; page 18: ©Album / Florilegius / Newscom; page 19: ©James R.D. Scott / Getty Images; page 21: ©UniversalImagesGroup / Contributor / Getty Images; page 22: ©Universal History Archive / Contributor / Getty Images; page 23: ©MOF / Getty Images; page 24: ©Martin Harvey / Getty Images; page 25: ©KAZUHIRO NOGI / Staff / Getty Images; page 26: ©TONY KARUMBA / Stringer / Getty Images; page 27: ©zhaubasar / Getty Images; page 27: ©Natalia / 500px / Getty Images; page 28: ©rusm / Getty Images

Cover: ©Kseniya Lapteva / Getty Images; ©Leonello / Getty Images; ©Nuttaya Maneekhot / Shutterstock

Printed in the United States of America.

CONTENTS

Imagine an animal so massive that the ground shakes as it walks. It's twice as tall as a human and has **evolved** to live in extreme conditions. And it's not alone. It travels in herds made up of close family members. Is it an elephant from today, or a mammoth from thousands, or even hundreds of thousands, of years ago?

The woolly mammoth is gone, but their bones, fur, and fossils remain. By learning as much as possible about the animals of the past, we can help save their cousins who are still alive today. One of those ancestors is the Asian elephant.

evolve: to change gradually to fit an environment

TUSK TRUTHS

Woolly mammoths were still alive 1,000 years after the Pyramids at Giza were built in Egypt.

CHAPTER 1

MAMMOTH VS. ELEPHANT

Asian elephants and mammoths look alike. They also share a lot of the same **traits**.

Woolly mammoths were social creatures that lived in herds. Staying in a group was important to their survival. Mammoths worked together to raise their young and protect each other. Asian elephants live in similar family groups.

trait: a distinguishing quality or characteristic

The first woolly mammoth bones were found in 1728. But scientists thought they belonged to an elephant until 1799.

Both mammoths and elephants have legs like tree trunks. But their foot bones are more like a dog's. Large foot pads help them stand and run on their tiptoes. Elephant and mammoth feet are flat because of the pad. Toenails protect the pad from wear and tear.

Woolly mammoths roamed the planet during the Ice Age. This period of time began 2.4 million years ago and ended 11,500 years ago. The **tundras** across Europe, Asia, and North America were some of the coldest places on Earth. Temperatures could drop down to –58° Fahrenheit (–50° Celsius).

Woolly mammoths had two layers of thick fur. They even had fur in their ears. A layer of body fat kept them toasty too. Asian elephants live in warmer places. They have thin coats of hair. Even their skin is thin in some places.

tundra: a large, flat, treeless area with very cold weather and short growing seasons

THE BIGGER THEY ARE...

When diving into the past, one thing is clear—there were a lot of BIG animals. One was the American mastodon. This huge elephant-like creature lived throughout North America, from Alaska to Mexico. They stood 7 to 10 feet (2.1 to 3 meters) tall. Some male mastodons had two sets of tusks. Their teeth were pointed to help them eat twigs and shrubs.

American mastodons died out between 10,000 and 13,000 years ago. Scientists believe that people and the warming planet led to their **extinction**. The mastodons traveled farther and farther north to escape hunters and the heat. But in the end, they could not **adapt** fast enough.

extinction: when an entire species has died off

adapt: to adjust to new conditions

Woolly mammoths were huge. They could grow 13 feet (4 m) tall and weighed 6 to 8 tons (5.4 to 7.3 metric tons). Bigger bodies meant bigger body parts. The larger something is, the more energy it takes to stay warm. But ears, tails, and feet lose heat the fastest. Mammoths adapted by making their ears and tails shorter and smaller.

Asian elephants are as tall as mammoths but aren't as heavy. Weighing between 3 and 6 tons (2.7 to 5.4 metric tons), they are the largest mammal in Asia. They use their ears to control their body's temperature.

MEASURING UP

Woolly Mammoth, 13 feet (4 m) tall

Imagine having to find food under snow and ice. The woolly mammoth used its massive tusks to dig in the snow and search for food. Tundra grasses and tiny flowers called forbs kept them full. Scientists believe that when the forbs disappeared at the end of the Ice Age, the mammoth did too.

The Asian elephant grazes on grass too. They also eat bark from trees, roots, and leaves. Bananas and sugarcane are special treats. An Asian elephant can eat up to 330 pounds (150 kg) of food a day. Finding that much to eat can be a challenge. Elephants often have to travel a long way to get their next meal. Grazing might also take them to dangerous areas.

Giant grazing animals, like woolly mammoths, kept grasslands clean and free of dry grass and dead leaves. Dry plants could lead to forest fires.

Asian elephants spend about 75 percent of their day either eating or looking for food and water.

CHAPTER 2

AT RISK

There are many possible reasons why woolly mammoths went extinct. One possibility is that they ran out of food. Humans hunting mammoths for food could be another reason. Elephants today are at risk because they are killed for their tusks. Mammoths could have been hunted to extinction too.

Climate change is another possible reason mammoths died out. Woolly mammoths were designed to live in cold places. When the planet warmed, they might have overheated. They weren't able to adapt.

Scientists do not yet agree on whether humans affected the long-term survival of woolly mammoths.

TUSK TRUTHS
Asian elephants have much smaller ears than African elephants. Many scientists believe this trait was passed down from their cousins, the mammoth.
Ears are not the only difference between Asian and African elephants. Tusks, overall size, and head shape are a few others.

BACK FROM THE BRINK

The Sumatran elephant lives on the islands of Sumatra and Borneo. There are less than 3,000 left in the wild. Some think that there could be as few as 900. They are critically endangered. This means they face a strong possibility of extinction.

Since 2007, the Sumatran elephant has lost half of its population due to **deforestation**. Hungry and homeless elephants enter human villages and towns. They eat farm crops and destroy fences and property. The farm owners poison and shoot elephants to keep them away.

The Elephant Flying Squad keeps wild elephants away from humans. They use noise and lights to scare them off. Trained elephants help too. Wild elephants avoid them. Protecting the remaining Sumatran elephants is crucial to their survival.

deforestation: clearing wide areas of trees

Today, the woolly mammoth is no more. Asian elephants are still around, but they are at risk of dying out too.

When a species disappears, the whole environment changes. Elephants are especially important. As nature's engineers, they affect both the land and the other animals that live there.

Traveling elephant herds create paths through dense forests. Other animals use these paths. Elephants dig watering holes that other animals drink from. Asian elephants also eat trees and shrubs, keeping these areas from getting overgrown. The loss of elephants would be a disaster for the environment.

Elephants need to drink between 25 and 50 gallons (94.6 and 189.3 liters) of water each day.

Animals are less likely to become extinct if they adapt to environmental changes. Scientists believe that elephants evolved from a pig-sized animal called Moeritherium that lived around 40 million years ago. It lived in swamps and rivers. Over millions of years, its **prehensile** upper lip evolved into an elephant trunk. Its large teeth would become tusks. As the **climate** changed, elephant ancestors had to move to find new homes. Their legs got longer. Their bodies got bigger. Trunks and tusks came in handy for finding more food.

prehensile: capable of grasping

climate: the weather conditions in an area over a period of time

Moeritherium was first discovered at Moeris Lake in Egypt.

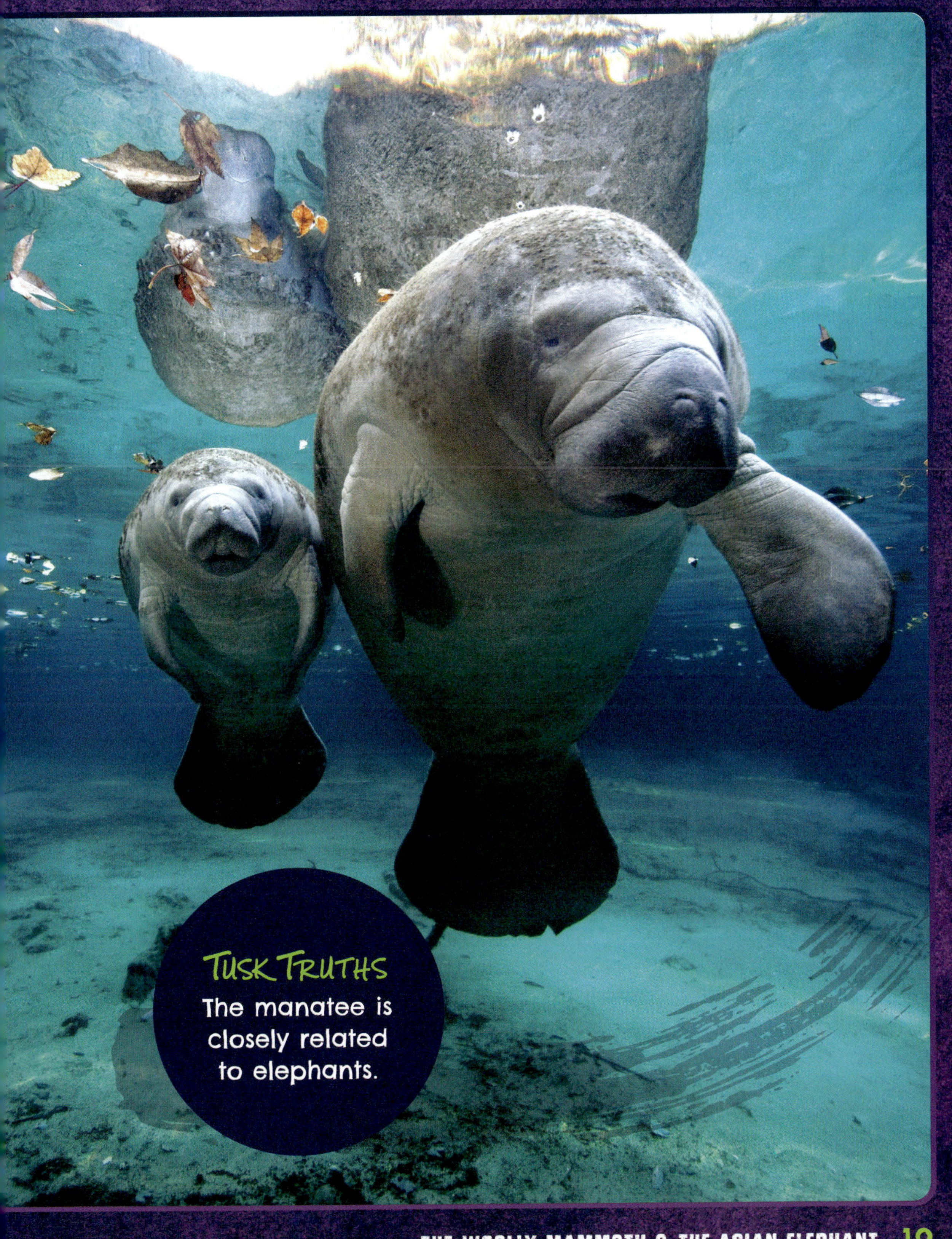

TUSK TRUTHS
The manatee is closely related to elephants.

PEOPLE: PROBLEM OR PROBLEM SOLVERS?

The oldest Asian elephant fossils ever discovered are 3 million years old. Modern humans have only been on the planet for about 200,000 years. We have never known a world without the elephant, and we have always lived alongside them.

Early humans hunted elephants for their meat and tusks. Later, the elephants' massive size served another purpose—weapons. Humans once trained elephants for wartime combat. Instead of horses, soldiers would ride elephants into battle. The sight of a charging elephant frightened soldiers.

War elephants could carry many soldiers and supplies. They could also crush enemies in their path.

Elephants have also been used for entertainment. For many years, people pictured elephants when they thought of the circus. However, training elephants can be a cruel process. Animal rights activists pressured the circus industry to change. After having elephants as part of their acts for more than 100 years, the Ringling Bros. Circus retired its last elephants in 2016.

Elephants are very smart. They have the largest brain of any land animal. They use tools and can identify languages. In addition, they have proven to show a wide range of emotions. They remember friends and mourn their deaths.

By the 1910s, the Ringling Bros. Circus had 26 elephants as part of their show.

Whether they are interacting with living or dying herd members, touch is important to elephants.

Because of humans, the elephant's future is at risk. Asian elephants are endangered. This means there is a high risk that they will become extinct in the future. It is estimated that there are less than 40,000 Asian elephants left. Around one-third of these live in **captivity**. The elephant population has dropped by more than 60 percent in the last decade.

captivity: held or confined by humans

Elephants are some of the most intelligent animals on Earth. Losing elephants would be a huge loss to the planet.

CREATIVE CONSERVATION

Sometimes scientists must think outside the box to save a species or ecosystem. De-extinction is one creative idea. It involves bringing an extinct species back to life. **Genetics** and **cloning** could lead to the return of lost species. In 1996, scientists were able to clone a sheep. Scientists are currently using the idea to bring back the woolly mammoth using frozen **mummified** remains.

Not everyone believes de-extinction is a good idea. Many conservationists think the money spent bringing animals back from extinction would be better used trying to save the ones that are in danger now.

genetics: the study of characteristics in an animal

clone: to copy

mummified: preserved

Humans are the biggest threat to elephants. Poachers hunt elephants for their skin, meat, and tusks. Tusks are made of ivory, which is used to make carvings and jewelry. Thousands of elephants are killed by poachers every year.

Laws have been put in place to protect Asian elephants. Organizations raise money to increase law enforcement in areas where elephants are hunted. Land has been set aside for them. People cannot hunt or live on these lands without permission.

While humans are a part of the problem, they can also be the solution. Knowing what makes elephants so special can go a long way in saving them. The woolly mammoth may be gone, but with education and conservation, the Asian elephant can be here for years to come.

In 2016, animal activists started the #WorthMoreAlive campaign. Their goal was to end elephant poaching and value the animal's life over anything else.

PREHISTORIC MAINSTAYS

Did you know that there are many prehistoric species still alive today? The Siberian musk deer has been around for more than 25 million years. It is also known as the vampire deer. The males don't grow antlers. Instead, they have fangs that can grow up to 4 inches (10.2 centimeters) in length.

Vampire deer were hunted for their **musk**, which is used in perfumes and colognes. Their populations are considered vulnerable. That means their populations are decreasing. Hunting them is illegal, but that doesn't stop poachers.

musk: a strong-smelling substance

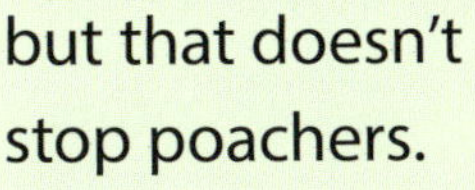

QUIZ

1 One difference between woolly mammoths and Asian elephants is:

    a. their trunks
    b. their diet
    c. their ancestors
    d. their legs

2 Critically endangered means:

    a. that there is a strong possibility a species will go extinct
    b. that there is a strong possibility that the species is already extinct
    c. that it is important that a species is endangered
    d. that people are skeptical that a species is endangered

3 Poachers hunt elephants for:

    a. their skin
    b. their tusks
    c. their meat
    d. all of the above

4 There are fewer than _______ Asian elephants left in the wild.

    a. 1 million
    b. 300,000
    c. 40,000
    d. 900

Key: 1) b; 2) a; 3) d; 4) c

BRUSH THOSE TUSKS PROJECT

Elephants have long tusks. Imagine having to brush something that big twice a day! Get a sense of just how much toothpaste you'd need to clean those chompers. Try this fun science experiment and make a mammoth-sized amount of toothpaste.

WHAT YOU NEED

- safety goggles
- funnel
- 20-volume hydrogen peroxide*
- 16-ounce (0.5 L) empty plastic bottle
- food coloring
- foil cake pan
- 1 tablespoon (15 milliliters) of dry yeast
- 3 tablespoons (45 mL) of warm water
- small cup

This 6 percent solution can be found in the beauty section of most stores.

STEPS TO TAKE

1. Put those safety goggles on!

2. Have an adult use the funnel to pour the hydrogen peroxide into the plastic bottle.

3. Add 8 drops of the food coloring into the bottle. Place the bottle in the cake pan.

4. Mix the dry yeast and water in the small cup. Have an adult pour the mixture into the bottle using the funnel.

5. Stand back and watch the mammoth toothpaste come to life!

GLOSSARY

adapt *(uh-DAPT)*: to adjust to new conditions

captivity *(kap-TIV-uh-tee)*: held or confined by humans

climate *(KLY-muht)*: the weather conditions in an area over a period of time

clone *(KLOHN)*: to copy

deforestation *(dee-for-uh-STAY-shuhn)*: clearing wide areas of trees

evolve *(uh-VOLV)*: to change gradually to fit an environment

extinction *(ik-STINGKT-shuhn)*: when an entire species has died off

genetics *(juh-NET-iks)*: the study of characteristics in an animal

mummified *(MUM-uh-fyd)*: preserved

musk *(MUSK)*: a strong-smelling substance

prehensile *(pre-HEN-sy-uhl)*: capable of grasping

trait *(TRAYT)*: a distinguishing quality or characteristic

tundra *(TUN-druh)*: a large, flat, treeless area with very cold weather and short growing seasons

READ MORE

Chinsamy-Turan, Anusuya. *Dinosaurs and Other Prehistoric Life.* New York, NY: Dorling Kindersley Publishing, 2021.

Huddleston, Emma. *Asian Elephants.* Minneapolis, MN: Bearport Publishing Company, 2023.

INTERNET SITES

Save the Elephants—STE WildTracks
https://www.savetheelephants.org/ste-tracking-app/
Download the WildTracks app and track elephants thousands of miles away.

Woolly Mammoth
https://kids.nationalgeographic.com/animals/prehistoric/facts/woolly-mammoth
Learn more about the woolly mammoth from National Geographic Kids.

INDEX